contents

NZ, Canada, US and UK readers
Please note that Australian cup and spoon measurements are metric. A conversion chart appears on page 63.

ingredients from a chinese kitchen

bamboo shoots tender shoots of bamboo plants; available, canned, from supermarkets.

black beans, salted also known as chinese black beans; fermented and salted soy beans available from most Asian food stores. Chop before (or mash during) cooking to release flavour.

bok choy, baby also known as pak kat farang, shanghai bok choy, chinese chard or white cabbage; smaller and more tender than bok choy. Available from supermarkets and greengrocers.

capsicum also known as pepper or bell pepper. Discard seeds and membranes before use.

char siu sauce also known as chinese barbecue sauce; reddish paste with sweet, spicy flavour. Available at supermarkets and Asian food stores.

chinese barbecue pork also known as char siu; roast pork fillets with a sweet-sticky coating, available from Asian food and specialty stores.

chinese cooking wine also known as shaoxing wine; replace with pale dry sherry. Purchase from most Asian food stores.

chinese pancakes small pancakes made of flour and water; available in Asian food stores.

chinese sausages spicy, bright-red, thin, dried pork sausage. The meat is preserved by high spice content; can be kept at room temperature.

choy sum also known as pakaukeo or flowering cabbage. Long stems with light-green leaves and yellow flowers; eaten, stems and all. Available at supermarkets and Asian food stores.

cornflour also known as cornstarch, used as a thickening agent and for coating food.

fennel, seeds available whole and ground; have a strong aniseed flavour.

fish sauce also called nam pla or nuoc nam; made from pulverised, salted, fermented fish. Available at supermarkets and Asian food stores.

five-spice powder a fragrant ground mixture of cassia, clove, star anise, sichuan pepper and fennel seeds; available from supermarkets, Asian food stores or specialty spice stores.

gai larn (right) also known as gai lum, chinese broccoli and chinese kale, this vegetable is prized more for its stems rather than its coarse leaves. Available from supermarkets, Asian food stores and greengrocers.

garlic chives small, green, leafy, bulbless member of onion family. Garlic chive leaves are long, thin and flat with a garlicky taste; also known as chinese chive, nira or chinese leek.

ginger also known as green or root ginger; thick, gnarled root of a tropical plant.

gow gee wrappers rounds of dough, made from wheat flour and water, used to wrap around savoury fillings, which are then fried or steamed. Wonton wrappers can be substituted. Work with one wrapper at a time and keep the rest covered with a damp cloth to prevent them drying out.

green onions also known as scallion or (incorrectly) shallot; immature onions picked before the bulbs have formed; they have a long, bright-green edible stalk.

hoisin sauce thick, sweet Chinese barbecue sauce, made from salted fermented soy beans, onions and garlic. Used as a marinade or baste; available from supermarkets and Asian food stores.

kecap manis sweet, thick soy sauce; available from most supermarkets and Asian food stores.

mesclun salad mix of assorted young leaves, including baby spinach, mizuna and curly endive.

noodles

fresh rice: available in various widths or large sheets which are cut into desired width. Chewy and pure white, they require no pre-cooking.

hokkien: also known as stir-fry noodles; fresh wheat noodles resembling thick, yellow-brown spaghetti needing no pre-cooking before use.

thin dried rice noodles: dried noodles made from rice flour and water (vermicelli). Before use, soak in boiling water to soften. Also known as rice stick noodles.

thin wheat: extremely thin wheat noodle (see right), also known as somen; available dried or fresh.

oyster sauce made from oysters and their brine, cooked with salt and soy sauce then thickened; available from most supermarkets and Asian food stores.

peanut oil pressed from ground peanuts; most commonly used oil in Asian cooking because of its high smoke point (capacity to handle high heat without burning).

rice wine vinegar also known as rice vinegar; a colourless vinegar made from fermented rice and flavoured with sugar and salt. Available from some supermarkets and Asian food stores.

sambal oelek also spelt ulek or olek; spicy condiment usually made of chilli, shrimp paste, sugar and salt. Available from most supermarkets and Asian food stores.

sesame oil made from roasted white sesame seeds; a flavouring rather than a cooking medium.

shiitake mushrooms available both dried (see left, top) and fresh (see left, bottom). Remove woody stems from fresh shiitake before use; they possess a rich flavour and dense texture. Dried shiitake must be soaked in hot water to reconstitute before use in stir-fries and various one-pot dishes.

sichuan peppercorns also known as szechuan or chinese pepper; a mildly hot spice from the prickly ash tree. Although it is not related to the peppercorn family, small, red-brown aromatic sichuan berries look like black peppercorns and have a distinctive peppery-lemon flavour and aroma. Available from Asian food stores and specialty spice stores.

snow pea sprouts also known as mange tout ("eat all").

soy sauce made from fermented soy beans. Several variations are available in most supermarkets and Asian food stores.

spinach also known as english spinach and, incorrectly, silverbeet. Its tender green leaves are good uncooked in salads or added to soups, stir-fries and stews just before serving. Baby spinach leaves, young leaves mostly used raw in salads, are also available.

spring roll wrappers available in various sizes, fresh or frozen, from Asian food stores. Can be used for making gow gee and samosas as well as spring rolls.

sugar, brown an extremely soft, fine granulated sugar retaining molasses for its characteristic colour and flavour.

tofu:

fried: packaged pieces of soft bean curd which have been deep-fried until the surface is brown and crusty and the inside almost dry.

soft: delicate bean curd; does not hold its shape with overhandling.

water chestnuts resemble chestnuts in appearance, hence the English name. They are small brown tubers with a crisp, white, nutty-tasting flesh. Their crunchy texture is best experienced fresh, however, canned water chestnuts are more easily obtained and can be kept about a month, once opened, under refrigeration.

peking duck

2kg duck
¼ cup (60ml) honey, warmed
1 lebanese cucumber (130g)
8 green onions
16 chinese pancakes,
    warmed
sauce
⅓ cup (80ml) hoisin sauce
2 tablespoons chicken stock
1 tablespoon plum sauce

1 Wash duck; drain well. Tie string around neck of duck. Lower duck into large saucepan of boiling water for 20 seconds; remove from pan. Drain well; pat dry with absorbent paper. Tie string to refrigerator shelf and suspend duck, uncovered, over drip tray overnight. Remove duck from refrigerator; suspend duck in front of cold air from an electric fan about 2 hours or until skin is dry to touch.
2 Preheat oven to moderate. Tuck wings under duck. Place duck, breast-side up, on wire rack in large baking dish; brush entire duck evenly with honey. Bake, uncovered, in moderate oven 30 minutes; turn duck. Reduce heat to slow; bake, uncovered, about 1 hour or until tender.
3 Place duck on chopping board; remove skin. Place skin in single layer on wire rack over oven tray; bake skin, uncovered, in moderate oven about 10 minutes or until crisp and browned. Slice skin; slice duck meat.
4 Using teaspoon, remove seeds from cucumber. Cut cucumber and onions into thin 8cm strips. To serve, top warm pancakes with duck meat, crisp skin, cucumber, onion and sauce; roll. Eat with fingers.
sauce Combine ingredients in small bowl; mix well.

serves 4
per serving 107.2g fat; 5935kJ (1420 cal)
tips The duck must be prepared a day ahead and refrigerated, uncovered.
Cooked duck can also be purchased from Chinese barbecue shops and some restaurants.

steamed chicken gow gees

2 dried shiitake mushrooms
500g minced chicken
2 green onions,
   chopped finely
1 tablespoon finely chopped
   fresh garlic chives
2 cloves garlic, crushed
2 teaspoons grated
   fresh ginger
¼ teaspoon five-spice
   powder
¾ cup (75g) packaged
   breadcrumbs
2 tablespoons hoisin sauce
1 teaspoon sesame oil
1 egg, beaten lightly
30 gow gee wrappers
1 tablespoon char siu sauce
1 tablespoon light soy sauce
2 tablespoons water
2 teaspoons sweet
   chilli sauce

1 Place mushrooms in small heatproof bowl; cover with boiling water. Stand 20 minutes; drain. Discard stems; chop caps finely.
2 Combine mushrooms, chicken, onion, chives, garlic, ginger, five-spice, breadcrumbs, hoisin sauce, oil and egg in large bowl. Roll level tablespoons of chicken mixture into balls (you will have 30 balls); place on trays. Cover; refrigerate 30 minutes.
3 Brush one wrapper with a little water; top with a chicken ball. Pleat wrapper firmly around ball. Repeat with remaining chicken balls and wrappers. Place gow gees in single layer, about 2cm apart, in baking-paper-lined bamboo steamer. Cook, covered, over large wok or frying pan of simmering water about 8 minutes or until gow gees are cooked through.
4 Combine remaining ingredients in small bowl. Serve as a dipping sauce with steamed gow gees.

makes 30
per gow gee 2g fat; 243kJ (58 cal)

oven-baked spring rolls

2 dried shiitake mushrooms
2 teaspoons peanut oil
1 green onion, sliced thinly
1 clove garlic, crushed
250g pork mince
2 tablespoons finely chopped
    water chestnuts
50g chinese cabbage,
    shredded finely
1 teaspoon fish sauce
2 teaspoons light soy sauce
1 tablespoon oyster sauce
24 small spring roll wrappers
1 egg, beaten lightly
chilli dipping sauce
2 tablespoons chinese
    red wine vinegar
2 tablespoons sweet
    chilli sauce

1 Place mushrooms in small heatproof bowl, cover with boiling water; stand 20 minutes, drain. Slice mushrooms thinly.
2 Meanwhile, heat oil in medium wok; stir-fry onion and garlic until onion softens. Add pork; stir-fry until browned and cooked through. Add mushrooms, water chestnuts, cabbage and sauces; stir-fry until cabbage wilts. Cool.
3 Preheat oven to moderately hot. Lightly oil oven trays.
4 Spoon filling onto centre of wrappers; brush edges with egg. Roll each wrapper on the diagonal to enclose filling, folding in sides after first complete turn. Place spring rolls on prepared trays, seam-side down; brush all over with remaining egg. Bake, uncovered, in moderately hot oven about 10 minutes or until browned lightly and crisp.
5 Serve hot with dipping sauce.
chilli dipping sauce Combine ingredients in small bowl.

makes 24
per roll 1.3g fat; 155kJ (37 cal)
per tablespoon sauce 0.3g fat; 54kJ (13 cal)
tips The pork filling can be cooked and the dipping sauce made a day ahead. Store separately, covered, in the refrigerator.

pork and chicken sang choy bow

500g pork fillets
⅓ cup (80ml) char siu sauce
1 tablespoon peanut oil
150g chicken mince
1 clove garlic, crushed
100g fresh shiitake
   mushrooms,
   chopped finely
190g can water chestnuts,
   rinsed, drained,
   chopped finely
2 green onions,
   chopped finely
2 tablespoons oyster sauce
1 tablespoon soy sauce
1 teaspoon sesame oil
1½ cups (120g) bean sprouts
8 large iceberg lettuce leaves
2 green onions, sliced thinly

1 Preheat oven to moderate.

2 Place pork on wire rack in large shallow baking dish; brush all over with ¼ cup of the char siu sauce. Roast, uncovered, in moderate oven about 40 minutes or until cooked as desired, brushing occasionally with pan drippings. Cool 10 minutes; chop pork finely.

3 Meanwhile, heat peanut oil in wok; stir-fry chicken, garlic and mushrooms for 5 minutes. Add water chestnuts, chopped onion, sauces, sesame oil, pork and remaining char siu sauce; stir-fry until chicken is cooked through. Remove from heat; add sprouts, toss sang choy bow gently to combine.

4 Divide lettuce leaves among serving plates; spoon sang choy bow into leaves, sprinkle each with sliced onion.

serves 4
per serving 13.4g fat; 1430kJ (342 cal)
tip An easy way to separate whole lettuce leaves is to rap the head of the lettuce, stem-end down, on a hard surface to loosen the core. Discard the core, and run a strong stream of cold water into the cavity – the leaves will fall away, intact. Submerge the leaves in iced water until ready to serve; use the lettuce centre for a salad.

combination noodle soup

500g chicken breast fillets
2 litres (8 cups) chicken stock
1 tablespoon light soy sauce
125g fresh thin wheat noodles
100g small cooked shelled prawns
200g chinese barbecued pork, sliced thinly
1¼ cups (100g) bean sprouts
4 green onions, sliced

1 Poach chicken in simmering water about 15 minutes or
until cooked through.
2 Remove chicken from pan using a slotted spoon; when cool
enough to handle, slice chicken thinly.
3 Combine stock and soy sauce in large saucepan, cover;
bring to a boil.
4 Add noodles to boiling stock; using tongs or a large metal fork,
immediately separate the strands. Reduce heat, add chicken, prawns,
pork, sprouts and onion to pan; simmer soup until heated through.
5 Using tongs, lift noodles from soup; divide among serving bowls.
Ladle remaining soup over noodles.

serves 4
per serving 14.9g fat; 1563kJ (374 cal)

hot and sour soup

1.25 litres (5 cups)
   chicken stock
3 cups (750ml) water
1 clove garlic, crushed
2 teaspoons grated fresh ginger
1 tablespoon sambal oelek
2 tablespoons light soy sauce
100g pork fillets, sliced thinly
100g chicken tenderloins,
   sliced thinly
8 fresh shiitake mushrooms,
   sliced thinly
½ cup (100g) drained canned
   bamboo shoots
2 tablespoons sake
⅓ cup (80ml) lime juice
1 teaspoon cracked
   black pepper
2 tablespoons cornflour
2 tablespoons water, extra
3 eggs, beaten lightly
300g soft tofu,
   chopped coarsely
4 green onions, sliced thinly

1 Combine stock and the water in large saucepan; bring to a boil. Stir in garlic, ginger, sambal and sauce; simmer, uncovered, about 3 minutes or until fragrant.
2 Add pork, chicken, mushrooms, bamboo shoots, sake, juice and pepper; bring to a boil. Reduce heat; simmer, uncovered, about 5 minutes or until meat is cooked through.
3 Blend cornflour with the extra water; add to stock mixture. Cook, stirring, until mixture boils and thickens slightly.
4 Gradually add egg, in a thin stream, to simmering soup, stirring continuously. Divide tofu and onion among bowls; ladle hot soup over.

serves 4
per serving 19.6g fat; 1491kJ (357 cal)
tips Replace the sambal oelek with fresh red chillies, if you prefer. If fresh shiitake mushrooms are unavailable, use button mushrooms or reconstituted dried shiitake mushrooms.

chicken and corn soup

2 teaspoons peanut oil
2 green onions, sliced finely
1 clove garlic, crushed
1 litre (4 cups) chicken stock
1 litre (4 cups) water
170g chicken breast fillets, chopped finely
310g can creamed corn
310g can corn kernels
1 tablespoon cornflour
¼ cup (60ml) water, extra
1 egg, beaten lightly

1 Heat oil in large saucepan; cook onion and garlic, stirring, until onion softens.
2 Add stock and the water to onion mixture; bring to a boil. Reduce heat, add chicken; simmer, uncovered, about 5 minutes or until chicken is cooked through.
3 Add both corns, and cornflour blended with the extra water. Cook, stirring, until mixture boils and thickens slightly. Gradually add egg, in a thin stream, to simmering soup.

serves 4
per serving 8.1g fat; 1138kJ (272 cal)
tip You can make your own chicken stock, or you can use one of the commercially prepared versions available in supermarkets.

twice-fried sichuan beef

600g piece eye fillet,
　sliced thinly
2 tablespoons dry sherry
2 tablespoons soy sauce
1 teaspoon brown sugar
½ cup (75g) cornflour
1½ cups (300g) jasmine rice
vegetable oil, for deep-frying
2 teaspoons sesame oil
1 clove garlic, crushed
1 fresh red thai chilli,
　chopped finely
1 medium brown onion
　(150g), sliced thickly
1 medium carrot (120g),
　halved, sliced thinly
1 small red capsicum (150g),
　sliced thinly
500g gai larn,
　chopped coarsely
1 tablespoon cracked
　sichuan peppercorns
2 tablespoons oyster sauce
¼ cup (60ml) soy sauce, extra
½ cup (125ml) beef stock
2 teaspoons brown
　sugar, extra

1 Combine beef, sherry, soy sauce and sugar in medium bowl. Stand 10 minutes; drain. Toss fillet in cornflour; shake off excess.

2 Meanwhile, cook rice in large saucepan of boiling water, uncovered, until just tender; drain. Cover to keep warm.

3 Heat vegetable oil in wok; deep-fry beef, in batches, until crisp. Drain on absorbent paper. Reserve oil for another use.

4 Heat sesame oil in same cleaned wok; stir-fry garlic, chilli and onion until onion softens. Add carrot and capsicum; stir-fry until just tender. Add gai larn; stir-fry until just wilted. Add beef with peppercorns, oyster sauce, extra soy sauce, stock and extra sugar; stir-fry until heated through. Serve beef and vegetables with rice.

serves 4
per serving 20.5g fat; 3046kJ (728 cal)
tip It is easier to slice the beef thinly if it is partially frozen.

honey prawns

1.5kg large uncooked prawns
1 cup (150g) self-raising flour
1¼ cups (310ml) water
1 egg, beaten lightly
½ cup (75g) cornflour
vegetable oil, for deep-frying
2 teaspoons peanut oil
¼ cup (90g) honey
100g snow pea sprouts
2 tablespoons sesame seeds, toasted

1 Shell and devein prawns, leaving tails intact. Sift self-raising flour into medium bowl; gradually whisk in the water and egg until batter is smooth. Just before serving, coat prawns in cornflour, shake off excess; dip into batter, one at a time, draining away excess.
2 Heat vegetable oil in wok; deep-fry prawns, in batches, until browned lightly. Drain on absorbent paper.
3 Heat peanut oil in same cleaned wok; heat honey, uncovered, until bubbling. Add prawns; coat with honey mixture. Serve prawns on snow pea sprouts, sprinkled with seeds.

serves 4
per serving 26.7g fat; 2654kJ (635 cal)

sticky pork spare ribs

1.5kg pork spare ribs, chopped
1 tablespoon peanut oil
¼ cup (60ml) char siu sauce
2 tablespoons soy sauce
2 tablespoons sweet chilli sauce
2 cloves garlic, crushed
2 teaspoons grated fresh ginger
¼ cup (90g) honey
⅓ cup (75g) firmly packed brown sugar
¼ teaspoon five-spice powder
¼ cup (60ml) dry sherry

1 Cook spare ribs in large saucepan of boiling water,
uncovered, about 10 minutes or until just cooked; drain,
pat dry on absorbent paper.
2 Heat oil in wok; stir-fry spare ribs, in batches, until browned
all over and cooked through. Drain spare ribs on absorbent paper.
3 Drain oil from wok. Add remaining ingredients to wok; bring
to a boil. Add spare ribs; stir-fry about 10 minutes, tossing until
pork is well coated in thickened sauce.

serves 4
per serving 23g fat; 2168kJ (519 cal)

lemon chicken

*This Southern Chinese speciality can be baked to reduce
the fat content.*

4 single chicken breast fillets (680g)
2 egg whites, beaten lightly
½ cup (75g) plain flour
30g butter
2 tablespoons vegetable oil
1½ tablespoons cornflour
1 tablespoon brown sugar
½ cup (125ml) lemon juice
½ teaspoon grated fresh ginger
1 teaspoon soy sauce
1 cup (250ml) chicken stock

1 Using a meat mallet, gently pound chicken between sheets
of plastic wrap until 1cm thick.
2 Dip chicken in egg white. Coat in flour; shake off excess.
3 Heat butter and oil in large frying pan; cook chicken, in batches, until
browned both sides and cooked through. Drain on absorbent paper.
4 Meanwhile, blend cornflour and sugar with juice in small saucepan.
Add ginger, sauce and stock; bring to a boil, stirring, until sauce
boils and thickens.
5 Slice chicken; serve drizzled with sauce.

serves 4
per serving 25.3g fat; 2011kJ (481 cal)
serving suggestion Top with shredded lemon rind and serve with
lemon slices and a bowl of fried or steamed rice.

salt and pepper squid

In China, this dish is usually enjoyed as a starter but, when you add boiled rice and wilted Asian greens, it makes a substantial main meal.

500g squid hoods
¾ cup (110g) plain flour
1 tablespoon salt
2 tablespoons ground black pepper
vegetable oil, for deep-frying
150g mesclun
chilli dressing
½ cup (125ml) sweet chilli sauce
1 teaspoon fish sauce
¼ cup (60ml) lime juice
1 clove garlic, crushed

1 Cut squid in half lengthways; score inside surface of each piece. Cut into 2cm-wide strips.
2 Combine flour, salt and pepper in large bowl; add squid. Coat in flour mixture; shake off excess.
3 Heat oil in wok or large saucepan; deep-fry squid, in batches, until tender and browned all over, drain on absorbent paper.
4 Serve squid on mesclun with chilli dressing, and lime wedges, if desired.
chilli dressing Combine ingredients in screw-top jar; shake well.

serves 4
per serving 12.2g fat; 1375kJ (329 cal)
tip Place flour, salt and pepper in a strong plastic bag with squid; hold the bag tightly closed, then gently shake to coat the squid in flour mixture. Remove squid from bag, shaking off any excess flour.

cantonese beef stir-fry

600g fresh rice noodles
2 tablespoons peanut oil
750g beef fillet, sliced thinly
1 teaspoon finely grated
   orange rind
1 tablespoon grated
   fresh ginger
2 cloves garlic, crushed
2 cups (170g) broccoli florets
1 large red capsicum (350g),
   chopped coarsely
1 tablespoon cornflour
½ cup (125ml) beef stock
10 fresh shiitake mushrooms,
   sliced thinly
½ cup (125ml) light soy sauce
⅓ cup (80ml) plum sauce
1 tablespoon brown sugar
3 cups (210g) coarsely
   shredded cabbage

1 Rinse noodles under hot running water; drain. Transfer to large bowl; separate noodles with fork.
2 Heat half of the oil in wok; stir-fry beef, in batches, until browned all over.
3 Heat remaining oil in wok; cook rind, ginger and garlic, stirring, until fragrant. Add broccoli and capsicum; cook, stirring, until just tender.
4 Blend cornflour and stock in small bowl; add to wok with beef, mushrooms, combined sauces and sugar. Bring to a boil; reduce heat. Cook, stirring, until sauce thickens slightly. Add noodles and cabbage; cook, stirring, until cabbage just wilts.

serves 4
per serving 19.9g fat; 3064kJ (733 cal)
tip Hokkien or fresh wheat noodles can be used in place of fresh rice noodles – but be sure to check the manufacturer's instructions regarding their preparation.

mongolian garlic lamb

700g lamb fillets, sliced thinly
3 cloves garlic, crushed
¼ cup (60ml) soy sauce
⅓ cup (80ml) sweet sherry
1 tablespoon cornflour
2 tablespoons vegetable oil
1 tablespoon brown sugar
1 teaspoon sesame oil
8 green onions, sliced thinly

1 Combine lamb, garlic, half of the sauce, half of the sherry
and cornflour in large bowl; mix well. Heat vegetable oil in wok;
stir-fry lamb mixture, in batches, until browned all over.
2 Return lamb mixture to wok. Add remaining sauce, remaining
sherry, sugar and sesame oil; stir-fry until sauce boils and
thickens slightly. Remove from heat; stir in onion. Serve on
a bed of stir-fried baby bok choy and steamed rice, if desired.

serves 4
per serving 16.8g fat; 1486kJ (355 cal)

chicken and almond stir-fry

2 tablespoons peanut oil
1 cup (160g) blanched whole almonds
600g chicken tenderloins
1 teaspoon grated fresh ginger
2 tablespoons hoisin sauce
1 small leek (200g), sliced thickly
200g green beans, halved
2 green onions, chopped finely
1 tablespoon soy sauce
1 tablespoon plum sauce
1 teaspoon sesame oil

1 Heat half of the peanut oil in wok; stir-fry almonds until browned, remove from wok.
2 Stir-fry chicken in wok, in batches, until browned and just cooked through.
3 Heat remaining peanut oil in wok, add ginger; stir-fry until fragrant. Add hoisin sauce, leek and beans; stir-fry until beans are just tender.
4 Return chicken to wok with onion, soy sauce, plum sauce and sesame oil; stir-fry until heated through. Toss through almonds.

serves 4
per serving 41.5g fat; 2466kJ (590 cal)

crab in black bean sauce

2 x 1.5kg uncooked mud crabs
1½ tablespoons packaged salted black beans
1 tablespoon peanut oil
1 clove garlic, crushed
1 teaspoon grated fresh ginger
½ teaspoon sambal oelek
1 tablespoon light soy sauce
1 teaspoon sugar
1 tablespoon chinese cooking wine
¾ cup (180ml) chicken stock
2 green onions, sliced lengthways

1 Place live crabs in freezer for at least 2 hours; this is the most humane way to kill a crab. Slide a sharp, strong knife under top of shell at back of each crab; lever off shell and discard.
2 Remove and discard gills; wash crabs thoroughly. Using cleaver, chop body into quarters. Remove claws and nippers; chop nippers into large pieces.
3 Rinse beans well under cold running water; drain. Lightly mash beans. Heat oil in wok; stir-fry garlic, ginger and sambal until fragrant. Add beans, sauce, sugar, wine and stock; bring to a boil.
4 Add all of the crab; cook, covered, about 15 minutes or until crab changes colour. Place crab on serving plate; pour over sauce. Top with onion.

serves 4
per serving 7.1g fat; 1186kJ (284 cal)
tip Place the green onion strips in iced water for about 20 minutes to make onion curls, a classic Chinese garnish.

stir-fried seafood with asian greens

20 medium uncooked prawns (500g)
500g squid hoods
500g firm white fish fillets
1 tablespoon peanut oil
5 green onions, chopped coarsely
2 cloves garlic, sliced thinly
50g fresh ginger, peeled, sliced thinly
500g baby bok choy, chopped coarsely
500g choy sum, chopped coarsely
2 tablespoons soy sauce
2 tablespoons oyster sauce
1 tablespoon mild chilli sauce

1 Shell and devein prawns, leaving tails intact. Cut squid hoods in half. Score inside surface of each piece; cut into 5cm-wide strips. Cut fish into 3cm pieces.
2 Heat half of the oil in wok; stir-fry seafood, in batches, until lightly browned all over and cooked through. Heat remaining oil in wok; stir-fry onion, garlic and ginger until onion softens.
3 Return seafood to wok. Add bok choy, choy sum and combined sauces; stir-fry until greens are just wilted and heated through.

serves 4
per serving 9.8g fat; 1524kJ (365 cal)

twice-cooked duck

1.7kg duck
1 tablespoon peanut oil
2 cloves garlic, crushed
1 tablespoon grated
  fresh ginger
2 tablespoons sweet
  chilli sauce
¼ teaspoon five-spice
  powder
ginger sauce
3 cups (750ml) chicken stock
1 large orange (300g), peeled
50g piece fresh ginger,
  sliced thinly
2 tablespoons brown sugar
2 green onions,
  chopped finely
2 teaspoons cornflour
¼ cup (60ml) water

1 Place duck in baking dish. Bake, uncovered, in moderate oven about 1 hour or until tender; cool. Cut duck in half lengthways; remove and discard rib and back bones.
2 Combine oil, garlic, ginger, sauce and five-spice in small bowl; mix well. Place duck in shallow dish; brush five-spice mixture over duck. Cover; refrigerate 3 hours or until required.
3 Preheat oven to moderately hot. Place duck, skin-side up, on wire rack over baking dish. Bake, uncovered, in moderately hot oven about 45 minutes or until skin is crisp. Pour ginger sauce over duck; serve with bean sprouts, baby spinach, green onion and coriander, if desired.
ginger sauce Place stock, whole orange and ginger in medium saucepan; simmer, uncovered, about 30 minutes or until reduced to about 1½ cups (375ml). Strain; return strained sauce to pan. Add sugar, onion, and blended cornflour and water; stir over heat until mixture boils and thickens slightly.

serves 4
per serving 95g fat; 4316kJ (1033 cal)

seafood combination omelette

12 eggs, beaten lightly
4 green onions, sliced thinly
1 tablespoon vegetable oil
1 clove garlic, crushed
1 red thai chilli, seeded,
   sliced thinly
26 scallops, halved
400g small shelled
   cooked prawns
400g cooked crab meat
2 tablespoons light soy sauce
⅓ cup firmly packed
   fresh coriander
2 tablespoons coarsely
   chopped fresh mint

1 Whisk eggs and onion together in large bowl.

2 Brush medium heated non-stick frying pan with a little of the oil. Add a quarter of the egg mixture; swirl to cover base of pan. Cook, covered, about 3 minutes or until cooked through. Remove omelette; repeat with remaining egg mixture to make three more omelettes.

3 Meanwhile, heat remaining oil in wok or large frying pan; stir-fry garlic, chilli and scallops until scallops are cooked through.

4 Add prawns, crab, sauce and herbs; stir until heated through.

5 Divide seafood mixture among omelettes; roll to enclose filling. Cut each omelette in half diagonally.

serves 4
per serving 22.2g fat; 1956kJ (468 cal)
tip We removed the roe from the scallops, but it can be left intact, if you prefer.
serving suggestion Serve this omelette with fried rice and steamed Asian greens.

roasted pork belly with plum sauce

800g boned pork belly, rind-on
2 teaspoons salt
1 teaspoon olive oil
1 cup (250ml) water
1½ cups (375ml) chicken stock
2 tablespoons soy sauce
¼ cup (60ml) chinese
   cooking wine
¼ cup (55g) firmly packed
   brown sugar
2 cloves garlic, sliced thinly
15g piece fresh ginger,
   sliced thinly
1 cinnamon stick, crushed
1 teaspoon dried chilli flakes
⅓ cup (80ml) orange juice
6 whole cloves
1 teaspoon fennel seeds
4 plums (450g), cut into
   eight wedges
cucumber salad
1 lebanese cucumber (130g)
1 long green chilli, sliced thinly
⅔ cup coarsely chopped
   fresh mint
1 tablespoon olive oil
1 tablespoon lemon juice
1 teaspoon caster sugar

1 Preheat oven to moderate.
2 Place pork on board, rind-side up. Using sharp knife, score rind by making shallow cuts diagonally in both directions at 3cm intervals; rub combined salt and oil into cuts.
3 Combine the water, stock, soy sauce, wine, sugar, garlic, ginger, cinnamon, chilli, juice, cloves and fennel in large shallow baking dish. Place pork in dish, rind-side up; roast, uncovered, in moderate oven 1 hour 20 minutes. Increase oven temperature to very hot. Roast pork, uncovered, in very hot oven about 15 minutes or until crackling is crisp.
4 Remove pork from dish; cover to keep warm. Strain liquid in baking dish into medium saucepan, skim away surface fat; bring to a boil. Add plum, reduce heat; simmer, uncovered, about 15 minutes or until plum sauce thickens.
5 Meanwhile, make cucumber salad.
6 Serve thickly sliced pork with plum sauce and salad.

cucumber salad Using vegetable peeler, cut cucumber lengthways into ribbons. Place cucumber in large bowl with remaining ingredients; toss gently to combine.

serves 4
per serving 51g fat; 3010kJ (720 cal)
tip Take care that the pork rind doesn't touch the cooking liquid or the crackling won't crisp.

sweet and sour pork

750g pork fillets
¼ cup (35g) cornflour
440g can pineapple pieces
   in natural juice
vegetable oil, for deep-frying
1 tablespoon peanut oil
1 medium brown onion
   (150g), sliced thickly
1 medium red capsicum
   (200g), chopped coarsely
1 medium green capsicum
   (200g), chopped coarsely
1 trimmed stick celery (75g),
   chopped coarsely
2 tablespoons tomato sauce
2 tablespoons plum sauce
2 tablespoons light soy sauce
¼ cup (60ml) white vinegar
1 tablespoon cornflour, extra
¼ cup (60ml) chicken stock

1 Slice pork into 1cm-thick slices. Coat pork in cornflour; shake off excess.

2 Drain pineapple over small bowl; reserve juice and pineapple separately.

3 Heat vegetable oil in wok; deep-fry pork, in batches, until browned all over. Drain on absorbent paper.

4 Heat peanut oil in same cleaned wok; stir-fry onion until just soft. Add capsicums and celery; stir-fry until vegetables are just tender.

5 Stir in combined sauces, vinegar, and extra cornflour blended with stock and reserved juice; cook, stirring, until mixture boils and thickens.

6 Add pork and pineapple; stir-fry until heated through.

serves 4
per serving 19.5g fat; 1986kJ (475 cal)
tip Placing pork, wrapped in plastic wrap, in the freezer for about 1 hour makes it easier to slice.
serving suggestion Serve with steamed white long-grain rice and crisp prawn crackers.

wok-tossed greens with oyster sauce

2 tablespoons peanut oil
4 cloves garlic, chopped finely
500g flat mushrooms, sliced thickly
1 tablespoon sesame seeds
400g baby bok choy, quartered
600g choy sum, chopped coarsely
4 green onions, chopped coarsely
2 tablespoons light soy sauce
⅓ cup (80ml) oyster sauce
1 teaspoon sesame oil

1 Heat half of the peanut oil in wok; stir-fry garlic, mushrooms and seeds until mushrooms just soften. Remove from wok.
2 Heat remaining peanut oil in same wok; stir-fry bok choy and choy sum until just wilted. Return mushroom mixture to wok with onion, combined sauces and sesame oil; stir-fry until heated through.

serves 8
per serving 6.5g fat; 397kJ (95 cal)
tips You can use any leafy Asian vegetable you like in this recipe. Do not cook this recipe until just before serving.
serving suggestions Serve with a side bowl of sambal oelek to add some spice to this recipe.

vegetable and tofu stir-fry

This simple dish is a great option for vegetarians as it includes tofu instead of meat. We used vermicelli-style rice noodles in this recipe.

250g thin dried rice noodles
2 tablespoons peanut oil
2 cloves garlic, crushed
1 tablespoon grated fresh ginger
150g fried tofu
2 medium carrots (240g), sliced thinly
1 medium red capsicum (200g), sliced thinly
250g gai larn, chopped coarsely
1 tablespoon cornflour
1 tablespoon brown sugar
⅓ cup (80ml) oyster sauce
⅓ cup (80ml) light soy sauce
2 tablespoons mirin

1 Place noodles in medium heatproof bowl; cover with boiling water. Stand until just tender; drain.
2 Heat oil in wok; stir-fry garlic, ginger, tofu, carrot, capsicum and gai larn until vegetables are just tender.
3 Add blended cornflour, sugar, sauces and mirin; stir-fry until mixture boils and thickens. Add noodles; stir-fry until hot.

serves 4
per serving 12.5g fat; 1665kJ (398 cal)
tip Mirin is a sweetened rice wine used in Japanese cooking. It is sometimes referred to simply as rice wine, but should not be confused with sake, the Japanese rice wine made for drinking. You can substitute sweet white wine or sherry for mirin.

stir-fried gai larn

1kg gai larn, trimmed, chopped coarsely
1 tablespoon peanut oil
5 green onions, chopped coarsely
2 cloves garlic, crushed
2 teaspoons grated fresh ginger
2 tablespoons soy sauce
2 tablespoons oyster sauce
1 tablespoon fish sauce
¼ cup (60ml) kecap manis
2 tablespoons sesame seeds

1 Boil, steam or microwave gai larn until just tender; drain.
2 Heat oil in wok; stir-fry onion, garlic and ginger until fragrant.
Add gai larn and sauces; stir until heated through. Drizzle with
kecap manis; toss with sesame seeds.

serves 4
per serving 8.1g fat; 588kJ (140 cal)

cantonese spinach with almonds

2 teaspoons peanut oil
2 tablespoons rice wine vinegar
2 tablespoons soy sauce
2 tablespoons honey
1 clove garlic, crushed
1 teaspoon grated fresh ginger
1kg spinach
4 green onions, chopped coarsely
½ cup (40g) flaked almonds, toasted

1 Heat oil in wok, add vinegar, sauce, honey, garlic and ginger; bring to a boil.
2 Add spinach and onion; stir-fry until spinach is just wilted. Serve sprinkled with nuts.

serves 4
per serving 8.2g fat; 639kJ (153 cal)

combination fried rice

You will need to cook about 1⅓ cups (260g) long-grain rice
for this recipe.

2 teaspoons peanut oil
3 eggs, beaten lightly
1 tablespoon peanut oil, extra
2 cloves garlic, crushed
2 teaspoons grated fresh ginger
6 green onions, sliced thinly
4 cups cooked white long-grain rice
200g cooked shelled small prawns
200g chinese barbecued pork, sliced thinly
3 chinese sausages (100g), sliced thinly
¾ cup (90g) frozen peas, thawed
1 cup (80g) bean sprouts
2½ tablespoons light soy sauce

1 Heat half of the oil in wok, add half of the egg; swirl wok
so egg forms an omelette over base. Cook omelette until set;
remove, cool. Repeat with remaining oil and remaining egg.
Roll omelettes, slice thinly.
2 Heat extra oil in same wok; stir-fry garlic, ginger and onion
until fragrant. Add rice, omelette, prawns, pork, sausage, peas,
sprouts and sauce; stir-fry until heated through.
serves 4
per serving 26g fat; 2604kJ (623 cal)

hokkien noodle stir-fry

500g hokkien noodles
1 tablespoon peanut oil
1 teaspoon sesame oil
500g beef fillet, sliced thinly
1 medium brown onion
(150g), sliced thickly
1 clove garlic, crushed
2 teaspoons grated
fresh ginger
1 medium red capsicum
(200g), sliced thinly
1 medium green capsicum
(200g), sliced thinly
2 tablespoons lemon juice
2 tablespoons sweet
chilli sauce
1 tablespoon sesame
seeds, toasted
1 tablespoon finely chopped
fresh coriander
1 tablespoon finely chopped
fresh mint

1 Rinse noodles under hot water; drain. Transfer to large bowl; separate noodles with fork.

2 Meanwhile, heat both oils in wok; stir-fry beef, in batches, until browned all over.

3 Add onion, garlic and ginger to wok; stir-fry until onion softens. Add capsicums; stir-fry until just tender.

4 Return beef to wok with noodles, juice and sauce; stir-fry until hot. Stir in seeds and herbs.

serves 4
per serving 16.9g fat; 2154kJ (515 cal)
tips Place beef in the freezer for about 1 hour before using to make it easier to slice. Chicken or lamb can substituted for the beef, if you prefer.

chinese barbecued pork and rice noodle stir-fry

Chinese barbecued pork is available from Asian grocery stores and barbecued meat shops.

375g dried rice noodles
1 tablespoon sesame oil
1 clove garlic, crushed
1 fresh small red thai chilli, seeded, sliced thinly
350g mushrooms, sliced thickly
2 teaspoons cornflour
¼ cup (60ml) soy sauce
600g chinese barbecued pork, sliced thickly
1 tablespoon fish sauce
¾ cup (180ml) chicken stock
8 green onions, sliced thinly

1 Place noodles in large heatproof bowl, cover with boiling water, stand until just tender; drain.
2 Meanwhile, heat oil in wok; stir-fry garlic, chilli and mushrooms until mushrooms are just tender.
3 Blend cornflour with soy sauce in small jug. Add cornflour mixture to wok with pork, sauce and stock; stir until sauce boils and thickens slightly. Add noodles and onion; stir-fry until hot.

serves 4
per serving 29.1g fat; 2990kJ (714 cal)

combination chow mein

8 medium uncooked prawns (200g)
2 tablespoons peanut oil
250g chicken mince
100g chinese barbecued pork,
    sliced thinly
1 medium carrot (120g), sliced thinly
1 medium brown onion (150g),
    sliced thinly
2 trimmed sticks celery (150g),
    sliced thinly
1 medium green capsicum (200g),
    sliced thinly
100g button mushrooms,
    sliced thinly
2 cups (140g) coarsely shredded
    chinese cabbage
1 cup (80g) bean sprouts
3 green onions, sliced thinly
2 teaspoons cornflour
2 tablespoons light soy sauce
2 tablespoons oyster sauce
½ cup (125ml) chicken stock
2 x 100g packets fried noodles

1 Shell and devein prawns, leaving tails intact.
2 Heat half of the oil in wok; stir-fry prawns until just changed in colour. Remove prawns from wok; cover to keep warm.
3 Add chicken to wok; stir-fry until cooked through. Add pork; stir-fry until heated through. Remove from wok; cover to keep warm.
4 Heat remaining oil in wok; stir-fry carrot and brown onion until onion softens. Add celery, capsicum and mushrooms; stir-fry until vegetables are just tender.
5 Return prawns and chicken mixture to wok with cabbage, sprouts, green onion and blended cornflour, sauces and stock; stir-fry until cabbage just wilts and sauce boils and thickens. Serve on noodles.

serves 4
per serving 25.1g fat; 1829kJ (438 cal)
tips Chinese barbecued pork has a sticky, sweet coating made from soy sauce, sherry, five-spice and hoisin sauce, and is traditionally cooked in special ovens.
You can use soft egg noodles instead of crunchy noodles, if you prefer, but check the manufacturer's instructions regarding their preparation.

61

index

conversion chart

MEASURES

One Australian metric measuring cup holds approximately 250ml, one Australian metric tablespoon holds 20ml, one Australian metric teaspoon holds 5ml.

The difference between one country's measuring cups and another's is within a two- or three-teaspoon variance, and will not affect your cooking results. North America, New Zealand and the United Kingdom use a 15ml tablespoon.

All cup and spoon measurements are level. The most accurate way of measuring dry ingredients is to weigh them. When measuring liquids, use a clear glass or plastic jug with the metric markings.

We use large eggs with an average weight of 60g.

DRY MEASURES

METRIC	IMPERIAL
15g	½oz
30g	1oz
60g	2oz
90g	3oz
125g	4oz (¼lb)
155g	5oz
185g	6oz
220g	7oz
250g	8oz (½lb)
280g	9oz
315g	10oz
345g	11oz
375g	12oz (¾lb)
410g	13oz
440g	14oz
470g	15oz
500g	16oz (1lb)
750g	24oz (1½lb)
1kg	32oz (2lb)

LIQUID MEASURES

METRIC	IMPERIAL
30ml	1 fluid oz
60ml	2 fluid oz
100ml	3 fluid oz
125ml	4 fluid oz
150ml	5 fluid oz (¼ pint/1 gill)
190ml	6 fluid oz
250ml	8 fluid oz
300ml	10 fluid oz (½ pint)
500ml	16 fluid oz
600ml	20 fluid oz (1 pint)
1000ml (1 litre)	1¾ pints

LENGTH MEASURES

METRIC	IMPERIAL
3mm	⅛in
6mm	¼in
1cm	½in
2cm	¾in
2.5cm	1in
5cm	2in
6cm	2½in
8cm	3in
10cm	4in
13cm	5in
15cm	6in
18cm	7in
20cm	8in
23cm	9in
25cm	10in
28cm	11in
30cm	12in (1ft)

OVEN TEMPERATURES

These oven temperatures are only a guide for conventional ovens. For fan-forced ovens, check the manufacturer's manual.

	°C (CELSIUS)	°F (FAHRENHEIT)	GAS MARK
Very slow	120	250	½
Slow	150	275 – 300	1 – 2
Moderately slow	170	325	3
Moderate	180	350 – 375	4 – 5
Moderately hot	200	400	6
Hot	220	425 – 450	7 – 8
Very hot	240	475	9

Are you missing some of the world's favourite cookbooks?

The Australian Women's Weekly cookbooks are available from bookshops, cookshops, supermarkets and other stores all over the world. You can also buy direct from the publisher, using the order form below.

MINI SERIES £2.50 190x138MM 64 PAGES

TITLE	QTY	TITLE	QTY	TITLE	QTY
4 Fast Ingredients		Crumbles & Bakes		Noodles	
15-minute Feasts		Curries		Outdoor Eating	
30-minute Meals		Drinks		Party Food	
50 Fast Chicken Fillets		Fast Fish		Pasta	
After-work Stir-fries		Fast Food for Friends		Pickles and Chutneys	
Barbecue		Fast Soup		Potatoes	
Barbecue Chicken		Finger Food		Risotto	
Barbecued Seafood		Gluten-free Cooking		Roast	
Biscuits, Brownies & Biscotti		Healthy Food 4 Kids		Salads	
Bites		Ice-creams & Sorbets		Simple Slices	
Bowl Food		Indian Cooking		Simply Seafood	
Burgers, Rösti & Fritters		Indonesian Favourites		Skinny Food	
Cafe Cakes		Italian		Stir-fries	
Cafe Food		Italian Favourites		Summer Salads	
Casseroles		Jams & Jellies		Tapas, Antipasto & Mezze	
Char-grills & Barbecues		Kids Party Food		Thai Cooking	
Cheesecakes, Pavlovas & Trifles		Last-minute Meals		Thai Favourites	
Chinese Favourites		Lebanese Cooking		Vegetarian	
Chocolate Cakes		Malaysian Favourites		Vegetarian Stir-fries	
Christmas Cakes & Puddings		Mince		Vegie Main Meals	
Cocktails		Muffins		Wok	
				TOTAL COST	£

Photocopy and complete coupon below

Name _____

Address _____

_____ Postcode _____

Country _____ Phone (business hours) _____

Email*(optional) _____

* By including your email address, you consent to receipt of any email regarding this magazine, and other emails which inform you of ACP's other publications, products, services and events, and to promote third party goods and services you may be interested in.

I enclose my cheque/money order for £ _____

or please charge £ _____ to my:

☐ Bankcard ☐ Mastercard ☐ Visa ☐ American Express ☐ Diners Club

Card number | | | | | | | | | | | | | | | | | | |

Cardholder's signature _____ Expiry date ____ /____

To order: Mail or fax – photocopy or complete the order form above, and send your credit card details or cheque payable to: Australian Consolidated Press (UK), Moulton Park Business Centre, Red House Road, Moulton Park, Northampton NN3 6AQ, phone (+44) (01) 604 497531, fax (+44) (01) 604 497533, email books@acpmedia.co.uk. Or order online at www.acpuk.com
Non-UK residents: We accept the credit cards listed on the coupon, or cheques, drafts or International Money Orders payable in sterling and drawn on a UK bank. Credit card charges are at the exchange rate current at the time of payment.
Postage and packing UK: Add £1.00 per order plus 25p per book.
Postage and packing overseas: Add £2.00 per order plus 50p per book.
Offer ends 30.06.2006